THE GHOSTLY TALES OF THE FLORIDA PANHANDLE

For Mrs. Cox, my third grade teacher. She showed me that I could be a writer if I wanted to. And to the red-haired girl who used to visit the people next door to my aunt and uncle many years ago. I wish I could remember her name. She always told the creepiest stories!

And as always, for Melanie.

Published by Arcadia Children's Books
A Division of Arcadia Publishing, Inc.
Charleston, SC
www.arcadiapublishing.com

First published 2026
Manufactured in the United States

Designed by Jessica Nevins
Images used courtesy of Shutterstock.com; p. 16, 28, 76 Ebyabe, CC BY-SA 3.0, via Wikimedia Commons; p. 50 Michael Rivera, CC BY-SA 4.0, via Wikimedia Commons.

ISBN: 9781467196161
Library of Congress Control Number: 2025948427

Spooky America

THE GHOSTLY TALES OF THE FLORIDA PANHANDLE

THOMAS SMITH

Adapted from Haunted Florida Panhandle by Katlyn Jones

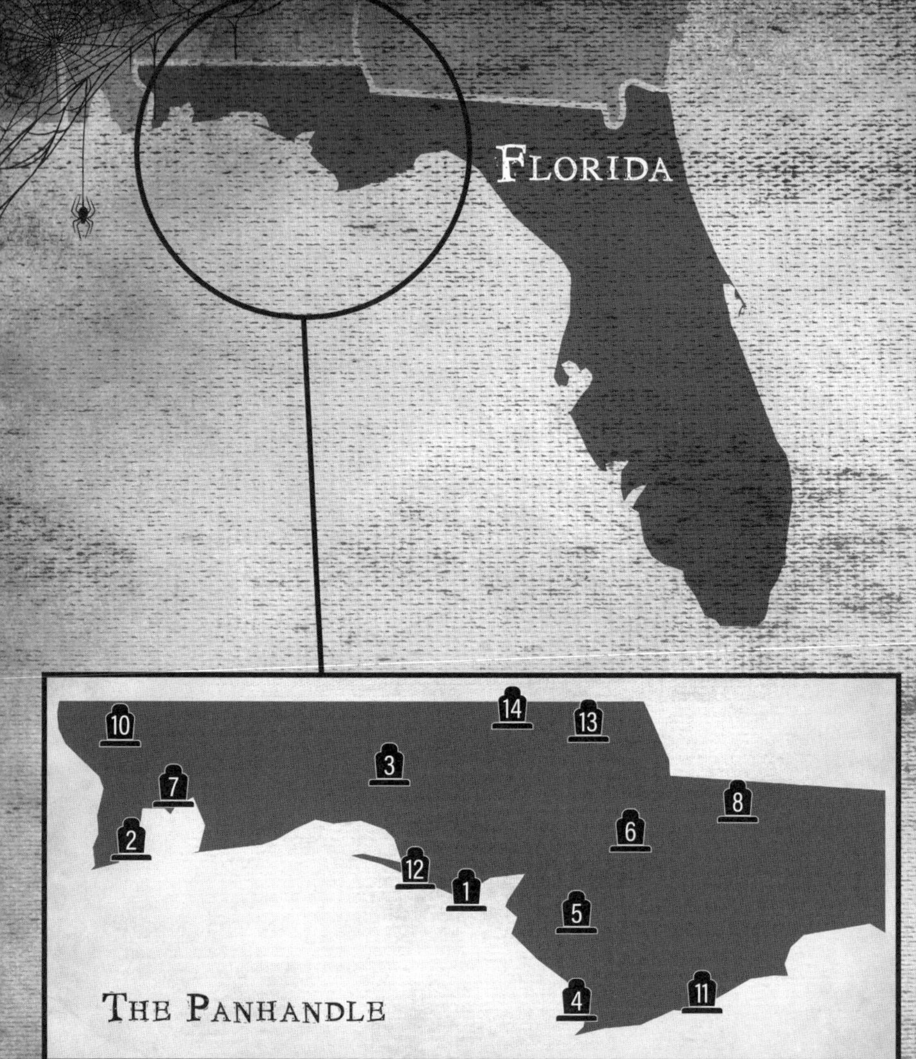
Florida
The Panhandle
10
14
13
3
7
8
2
6
12
1
5
4
11

Table of Contents & Map Key

St. Marks Lighthouse
St. Marks National Wildlife Refuge

Welcome to the Spooky Florida Panhandle!

Hello, fellow ghost hunters. Have you ever wondered how some places become haunted? Yeah . . . me too. Take the Florida Panhandle, for example. It's made up of thirteen counties that border what has been called the Forgotten Coast (sounds creepy already). The area has miles of natural beaches, barrier islands, fishing villages, historic districts, and popular beachside towns.

And despite its beauty, the Panhandle is one of Florida's best-kept secrets.

It's *also* one of the state's most haunted areas.

If you live somewhere long enough, you start to hear things. Strange things. Unsettling stories about lost loves, tragic events, disturbed burial sites, curses, betrayal, and murder. And if you mix all that together, the result WON'T be pretty. There is energy in each tragic event, and just like a battery, this supernatural energy is stored where the events occurred.

For example, in this beautiful vacation area along the southern borders of Alabama and Georgia, there are tales of a family, all murdered on the same night. There's a bar where poltergeist activity is a common occurrence. One story tells of the tragic demise (that means *death* for those of us who didn't always pay attention in English class) of a motel resident that even now causes alarms to buzz, televisions to turn on and off, and lights to flash at all hours. And as with many areas of the country, there are cemeteries in the Panhandle where some "residents" don't rest in peace . . . or at all.

Add to that the theater where mysterious footsteps, phantom applause, and lights that flicker sporadically with no cause are commonplace. A place where some of the spectral staff are still attached to the building includes the spirit of a former projectionist, and the ghost of an actress in white often seen gliding across the stage. For years, there was even a wax museum and horror-themed attraction called Castle Dracula in the area, and though it no longer exists, it's still the site of some of the strangest events in this collection. With so many unexplained events and tragic sites so close together, the Florida Panhandle can't help but be haunted!

Years ago, I was doing the same thing you're doing right now: reading a book of regional ghost stories. And that sparked my love of creepy stories of the supernatural. My friends Pam, Gene, and I would tell each other spooky stories, then we'd dare each other to visit the haunted McMasters place about a quarter of a mile down the dirt road near my house. And finally, late one summer afternoon (just about dusk), our collection of junior ghost hunters headed out on our first real ghost hunting adventure to explore the old house.

Yes sir, we made our way to that ramshackle place like a group of real paranormal investigators. Marched right up to the old house; its cracked windows staring down at us like the cataract-shrouded eyes of an evil witch. Every creak of the old manse (that's an old-fashioned word for "big old creepy house" or something like that) strengthened our resolve. One by one, we walked up the rickety steps, felt the sag and groan of every loose plank in the old porch floor, and headed to the front door, then, the deserted parlor beyond. Next, we . . . uh . . . we . . .

Okay, we ran down the dirt road, slowed down just long enough to touch the front porch steps, then ran double speed back to my house. Yelling and screaming the whole way. Just happy when we got back safe and sound without being grabbed by anything creepy.

So, who would have guessed that years later, one of those junior ghost hunters (me, in case you missed the name on the cover of the book) would actually go to haunted sites? Interview actual ghost hunters. Even come face-to-face with some of the supernatural phenomenon and cursed relics you and I like to read about? And who knows? You might be next to find a great publisher (like this one!) who wants to help you share your ghostly adventures.

Are you ready to hear about the ghostly and undead residents of Florida's Haunted Panhandle? Then let's start with the most unlikely site in the panhandle (or anywhere else in Florida). Let me tell you about *Castle Dracula*.

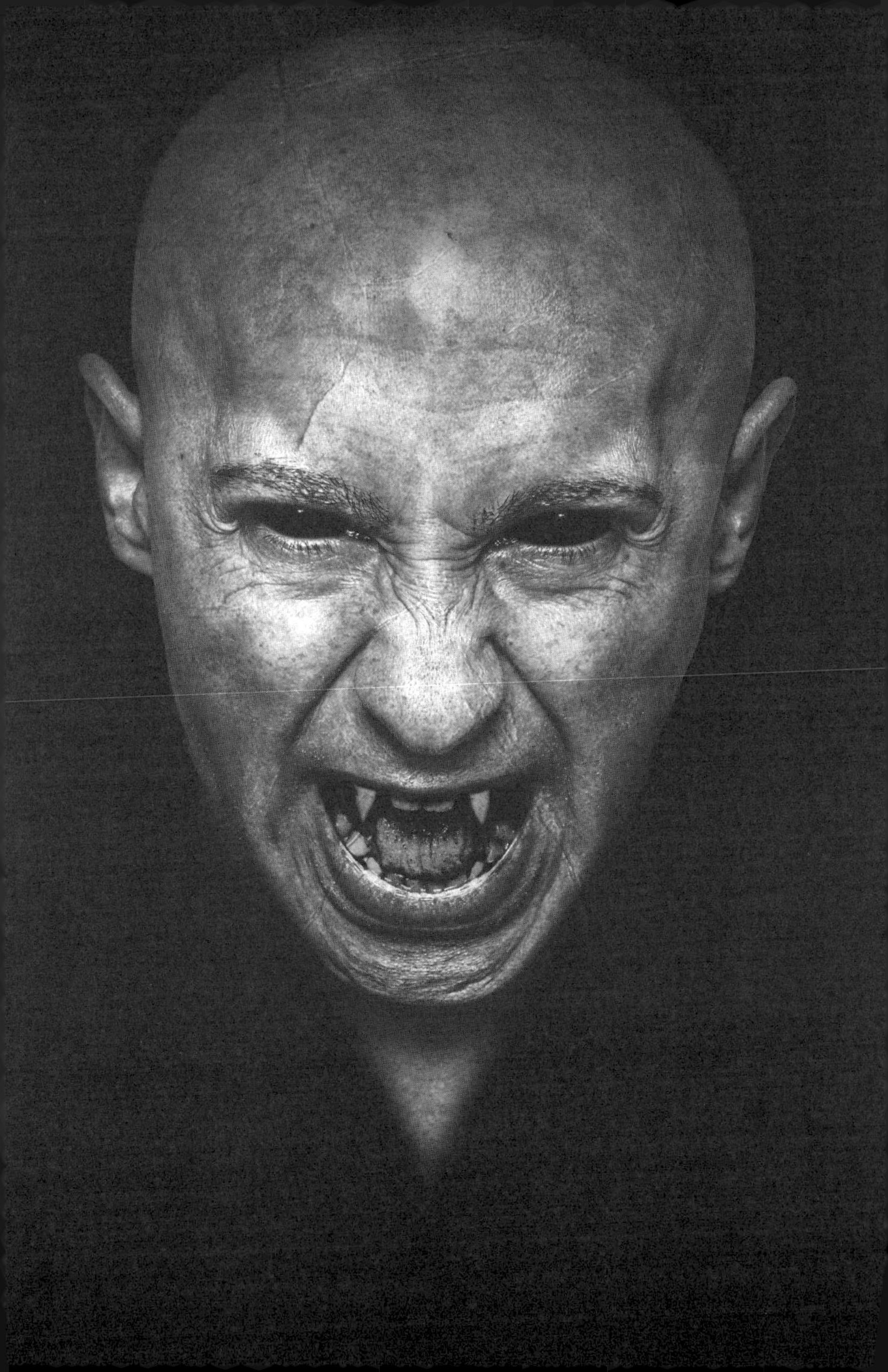

Castle Dracula

No, you didn't read that wrong. We're not in Transylvania. If you go looking for it, you'll find the location is now a seafood restaurant (they have great shrimp). But that hasn't always been the case. In the summer of 1976, Castle Dracula opened its doors to an unsuspecting public, and a gruesome legend was born. The massive black and white castle (part wax museum, part magic shop and gift shop) was unlike anything the locals and tourists had seen before.

There were mummies, phantoms, wolfmen, Dracula himself, and many other scary monster figures displayed in all their macabre glory. In addition to the various spooky scenes that were a major part of the experience, the castle even had an actual *undead celebrity* in residence.

The Frankenstein monster roamed the castle, frightening visitors and posing for photographs with his unsuspecting victims. Very few collections of vacation photographs from Panama City Beach in the late '70s didn't include at least one photograph of a grinning boy or girl in the "clutches" of Victor Frankenstein's evil creation.

However, Castle Dracula wasn't the only attraction in the area back then. There was also The Hang Out, Miracle Strip amusement Park,

Funland, Goofy Golf, Snake-A-Torium, Jungle Land, and Petticoat Junction Amusement Park. But Castle Dracula was on every kid's *I Gotta Do This* list.

Now some of you are probably saying, "Okay, that's great. But this is not a travel guide. What about the REAL scary stuff?" Well, I'm glad you asked. Because while the castle might have originally been created as a tourist attraction . . . something happened. And the effects of whatever it was are still being felt today. But don't take my word for it. Mike Smith, a resident of Panama City Beach back in those days, was an eyewitness to some of the uncanny events that turned the castle into a real house of horrors.

Mike and his younger brother, Sean, loved the castle with its life-sized monsters and scary scenarios. Or they did, until one particular day. They were making their way down the winding halls and eerie scenes when they came to the séance room. (A séance is a gathering where people try to communicate with the spirits of people who have died.) "The energy emanating from that séance room set the mood for the entire place," Mike said. But on one particular day, the mood was different. The brothers were excited at first—until they approached the room and noticed something unusual.

"You feel that?" Sean asked.

"Yeah," Mike said. "Something doesn't feel right.

The boys, both teenagers at the time, stood still. Listening. Trying to find anything familiar in this new and different vibe. But something was off. Sean wanted to stay a little longer, but Mike was anxious to leave. The room felt weird. And both boys felt a slight tingle running through their bodies. Like

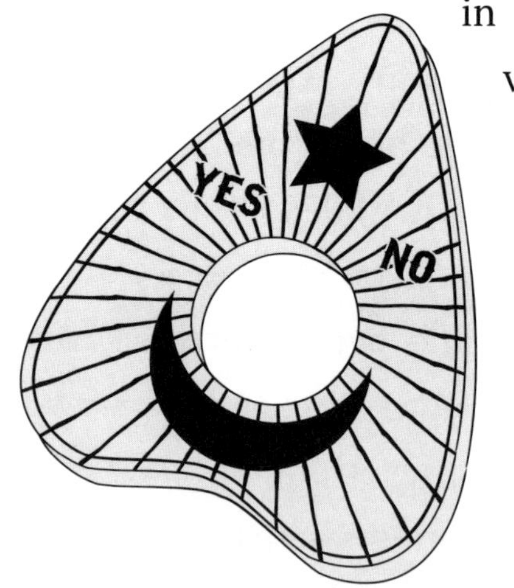

an icy hand sliding along their spines. Then, they heard the voice.

"Boys, come closer."

At first, unable to move, they looked around for the source of the voice. The room was not wired for audio, so that wasn't it. Their parents had already gone outside to wait for them, and there was nobody else in the room. They were alone . . . almost. A moment later, their paralysis broke and they headed for the exit. But not before the *something or somebody* tried to make contact one more time. Mike recalls the experience vividly.

"I heard a women's voice calling out," he said, "speaking right in my ear." He could feel a presence beside him. At that moment, they both ran out of the castle and found their parents in the parking lot. They pleaded with their mom and dad to take them away from there immediately. And later, even with their parents' reassurances, the two teenagers refused to return. They'd had enough of Castle

Dracula and whatever it was that walked the dark, twisting halls.

Mike said years later, in the summer of 1987, Castle Dracula burned down under mysterious circumstances. Nobody knows how or why. But the story doesn't end there. The castle might have been gone and the lot cleared, but something . . . *otherworldly* . . . remained. When a Wendy's was built on the site of the former haunted attraction, the something made that its new home.

Former employee, Paul Bonnette, experienced the same entity that had previously sent two teens running out, never to return.

Paul said things really came "alive" at night. More than once, he experienced supernatural manifestations at the restaurant. It always started slow; an occasional flickering light that could have been "just one of those things." But then they escalated. Drink machines would overflow and start dispensing their contents randomly. The flickering lights increased. And often, chairs, silverware, and other objects would mysteriously move to other parts of the restaurant, some of them hard to locate or reach.

Today, the space houses a seafood restaurant known for its friendly service and tasty shrimp. I wonder what "extras" they have on the menu?

Old Sacred Heart Hospital
Pensacola, Florida

Old Sacred Heart Hospital

Here's a trivia question for you: What is one of the oldest standing hospitals in the Florida Panhandle AND one of the most haunted locations in Escambia County? If you said Old Sacred Heart Hospital in Pensacola, you are correct. And if you didn't, here's an extra credit question: What hospital in the Florida Panhandle was built by nuns in 1915 (*hint: look at the title of this story*)? Did you guess Old Sacred Heart Hospital (you DID, didn't you)? Then you are one hundred percent correct!

The old Gothic Revival building stands on Twelfth Avenue, watching over the town like a stern schoolmaster. Before the hospital was built, the closest facilities available for serious medical issues were in Mobile, Alabama and New Orleans, Louisiana. So, the Sacred Heart Hospital was a welcome addition to the entire area. And after construction was completed, this was no ordinary hospital. It was the first facility in Florida to offer bacterial, surgical, radiological, and therapeutic facilities.

But the days when the hospital was used for its intended purpose are long gone. Overcrowding and the start of deterioration finally took its toll, and a new hospital had to be built in a different location to replace it. Even so, the building wasn't simply left and forgotten—just the opposite. The old hospital (added to the National Register of Historic Places in 1982) is home to businesses, restaurants, and even a school these days. And it's one of those restaurants that we need to focus on.

O'Zone Pizza opened in the former hospital building in 1998. Downstairs. Way downstairs, it opened in what used to be . . . the *morgue.* That's right. The place where they took dead people. As we all know, you can't open a business in a place where they used to store dead people without something strange happening. And sure enough, strange things started happening almost as soon as the restaurant opened.

The women's restroom, in particular, is said to be supernaturally active. Many people have heard whispering when there's no one in the restroom, and it is not unusual for the faucets to turn on and off by themselves. People often claim to see shadowy figures near (and even IN) the elevators. It has also been reported that the spirits of nuns who used to work in the hospital will tap visitors on the shoulder when no one else is around.

A waiter witnessed one very interesting event not so long ago.

Paul Sackman works at O'Zone Pizza, so he is very familiar with all aspects of the restaurant. On one particular night, as he was going about his closing duties for the evening, he stopped at the hostess station to make sure everything was in place and ready for the next day. He placed his notepad on the adjoining counter for just a moment when—WHAM!—an unseen hand swept it clean off the countertop. The pad flew through the air and slammed into the glass window by the front stairs . . . a full eight to ten feet away! Paul wasn't sure what had caused it, "but it sure had the employees on their toes," he said.

And finally, we come to what seems to be the story of a full manifestation. This chilling episode comes to us from a customer named Allie, who was at the restaurant celebrating her birthday with friends. While looking at the memorabilia on the back wall, the group turned toward the stairs. Suddenly, a man dressed in surgical scrubs materialized in front of them. He appeared to be enraged, and just stood there, staring at Allie and her friends. We may never know for sure if the mysterious man in scrubs was a ghost or not, but it sure makes you wonder who—or *what*—may be roaming the old building.

Hotel Defuniak

Ready for a story about a *Dead-and-Breakfast* spot? The Hotel Defuniak, built in 1920, has been a Masonic Lodge, a drugstore, a furniture store, and a bed-and-breakfast. (A bed-and-breakfast is a small hotel or inn, often in someone's home, where guests can stay overnight and have breakfast in the morning.) When the Hutchings family purchased the hotel in 2001, they decorated each of the rooms with European antiques, and a world class bed-and-breakfast destination was born. With only twelve rooms, Hotel Defuniak was often booked solid by locals and visitors passing through on their way to Walt Disney World. But these days, it has a more ominous distinction. In fact, some say it is one of the ten most haunted bed-and-breakfasts in Florida. And the reason it acquired that reputation is heartbreaking.

Generally, when you check into a hotel, you expect to come in at the end of the day, watch a little TV, maybe play a game or two, and settle in for a good night's sleep. And in most hotels, that's what happens. But not always in this one. Sometimes you might hear someone singing, but if you do, it might not be the kids in the room next door. It is probably the children in room No. 8 (also known as The Aviary Room).

That's the same room where two children drowned. And where a guest died after jumping out of the window.

Many guests and even the housekeeping staff have reported seeing a ghostly pair of young children, and a lamp that moves by itself. Some guests have talked about hearing strange sounds, and feeling the presence of something in the room with them.

Scott Clark is a former guest with an interesting story to tell. Scott had checked in and made his way to his room. Ready for a good night's sleep, he emptied his pockets, placed his phone on the television near the charging outlet, put his clothes away, and climbed into bed. Just moments before he drifted off to sleep, he heard a thud. He was so comfortable, he ignored the noise and went to sleep.

The next morning, however, he discovered the source of the thump in the night. There, in the middle of the floor, was his cell phone. Could it have slipped off the television and ended up in the middle of the floor? Scott says no. "My phone had a rubber casing around it that gripped any slick surface, and didn't slide."

Tonya Williams Welch stayed at the hotel with her husband, but they didn't know about the hotel's haunted history. She was just excited they managed to get a room (room No. 8, the last one available) late that night. They hadn't been in the hotel long when Tonya laughed and told her husband, "Wow, this place has got to be haunted." The owner confirmed that the hotel was indeed haunted, telling the couple some of its tragic history.

Later that night, a sound woke the couple from a deep sleep. They heard children giggling, and what sounded like jacks being thrown against the door. Most startling of all, they felt something

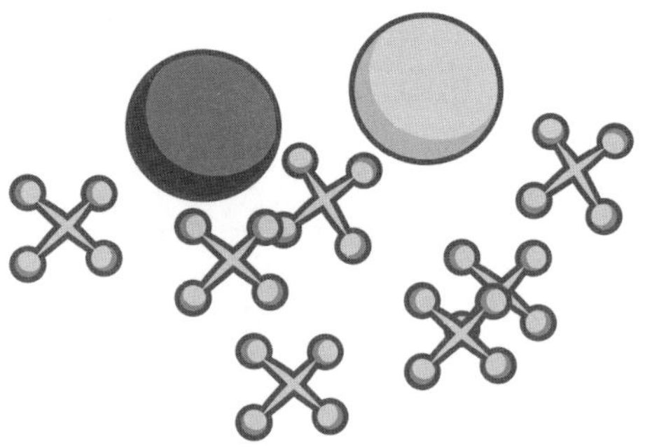

jumping up and down on the foot of their bed. And while they did not see the apparitions, they felt cold presences near them. Needless to say, they didn't get much sleep after that.

Now that you know about the hotel, let me ask you a question. Are you brave enough to stay in room 8?

Old Gulf County Courthouse
Wewahitchka, Florida

Gulf County Courthouse

For more than 150 years, Port Saint Joe has welcomed ships of all kinds to the Florida Panhandle. Named after the Gulf of Mexico, Gulf became a county in 1925. And two years later (1927 in case you don't want to do the math), the county's first courthouse was built in Wewahitchka, Florida (*Wewahitchka* is a Native American word meaning "water eyes"). Over the years, the county grew and prospered.

In 1933, Alfred I. Dupont bought the Apalachicola Northern Railroad. He hoped the railroad would ensure the future success of a papermill in the city of Port Saint Joe. But Mr. DuPont died in 1935, before he could see the completion of his dream. In an effort to see the plans completed, DuPont's brother-in-law, Edward Ball, created the Saint Joe Paper Company. Then he built the Saint Joe Papermill.

The company opened in 1938 and ran for over sixty years. In 1960, when the county needed a new courthouse, it was built in Port Saint Joe. And while the courthouse is still standing, it has a tragic history. One of the most tragic natural events was Hurricane Michael. In October of 2018, the Category 5 hurricane ripped through Gulf and Bay counties.

It was the third-most intense Atlantic hurricane to make landfall in the United States and the first Category 5 hurricane on record to impact the Florida Panhandle. The hurricane caused at least seventy-four deaths, including fifty-nine in the United States and fifteen in Central America. But Michael was just the beginning. Tuesday, July 28, 1987 brought another life-changing tragedy.

Clyde Melvin was in court for an alimony hearing on that fateful Tuesday. Judge W. L. Bailey was presiding over a property hearing between Melvin and his wife. When they went back into the judge's chambers, Melvin started yelling, then shooting in an adjoining conference room. He killed the judge and two other people before being wounded by a sheriff. He was charged with three counts of first-degree murder.

Locals say some of the people killed in that horrific event are still in the building, their souls anchored to the scene of the crime—and they *will* make their presence known. Sometimes they cause

the lights in the judge's chambers to flash on and off. Or they cause the elevator to work erratically. Staff member Jennifer Stanley has firsthand knowledge of the unusual events that occur in the courthouse. She has heard disembodied voices, and the sound of someone running on the catwalk that connects the courtroom to the jail.

What would you do if you heard those sounds?

Gulf Correctional Facility

We seem to be on a law-and-order roll. So, let's look where the idea of a life sentence takes on a whole new meaning: the Gulf Correctional Institution of Wewahitchka. Many correctional facilities are the scene of pain and suffering. Sometimes inmates have terrible fights. Sometimes they even die in their cells. Sometimes things are so bad, the correctional officers themselves are afraid. They have a very dangerous job. And while most people don't expect jails and prisons to be happy places, they also don't expect them to have a dark side like this one. But ever since its doors opened in 1992, inmates and guards alike have experienced too many weird things that just can't be explained.

Take correctional officer Benjamin Wilburn, for example. On the night he first encountered the uncanny, his shift started just like any other. Walking through the two-story confinement dorm, he passed Cell 101 on his left and Cell 112 on his right. Next to the cell on his right were four shower cells. Since the inmates had already showered and gone back to their cells to sleep, the hall was dark except for the shower cell lights.

Benjamin went to his desk somewhere between two and three o'clock in the morning to do his nightly paperwork. The area was quiet and everything was going smoothly like always . . . until it wasn't. Suddenly, he began to feel anxious. As he sat at his desk, the feeling of unease turned to dread. Then, he saw something out of the corner of his eye. A pitch-black mist was coming toward him from the dorm area.

The mist took the form of a man and started going slowly from cell to cell, moving silently into and out of each one. Benjamin was frozen, both fascinated and terrified by what was happening. When it was over, he contacted his sergeant and asked if he had ever heard of anything like that happening before. When his boss arrived, he expected the senior officer to laugh or question his eyesight, but the sergeant said something totally unexpected: "Oh, yeah. This place is haunted for sure."

While they stood talking, it happened again. And as soon as they both acknowledged its presence, the mist dissipated. Benjamin decided then and there that he didn't want to be in any one place for too long. He said, "Imagine how we feel right now; and imagine how the prisoners who have life sentences here feel. They must remain here within the jail, and that's terrifying."

Tanner Brown, another correctional officer, said nights when there is a full moon seem to be the worst. On one such night he was doing a perimeter check. As he rounded a corner of the building about midnight, he thought he saw another guard coming toward him. Nothing unusual in that . . . until the figure came closer. Then he saw it had *no face*. Tanner said his heart almost stopped. Then, when it was within about five feet of him, the ghastly figure dropped to the ground and disappeared.

Another time, Tanner Brown was in the prison dorm. He heard what sounded like someone being attacked inside one of the sections, so he opened the door and went in—but there was no one there. Suddenly, the door slammed behind him. And the guard wasted no time in grabbing the door, flinging it open, and getting out of the dorm.

A former captain of the Gulf Correctional Institute (who has asked to remain anonymous) said on one particular night, he felt like he had walked into a horror movie. He was doing his normal rounds, checking on the inmates, and when he came to the dorm closest to the end of the hall, he shone his flashlight in one of the windows . . . and his blood ran cold. Because there, near the bottom bunk, was a creature with glowing red eyes. It was squatting with its hands on the bunk, and it was staring straight at the captain. The captain looked away, tried to clear his head, and looked back into the room. To his horror, the creature shifted into a dark shapeless mass before suddenly hurling itself toward the door.

The captain ran from the area, scared out of his mind. He burst into the officer's station and tried to catch his breath and get control of himself. He was shaking uncontrollably. When he was finally able to speak, he told the other guards that he would NOT be going back to finish his rounds.

To be honest, I can't say I blame him. After all, could *you* have finished those rounds?

Old Calhoun County Jail

While we're on the subject of jails, here's another tale of the living incarcerated with the dead for you to ponder. This particular perplexing, petrifying prison is located in Calhoun County. The area is home to busy farms, beautiful scenic landscapes, and has a great rural vibe. But it is also home to one of the area's most haunted locations (what a surprise!).

The county was established in 1838 and named for U. S. Senator John C. Calhoun from South Carolina. Blountstown was named for the Seminole

Chief, John Blount. You might remember the chief from history class. He acted as a guide for General Andrew Jackson when he came to Florida and claimed it for the Spanish. In exchange for his help, the chief was given land for a reservation in 1823. The reservation thrived, but later, the government purchased the land from them and moved the reservation to another state. Still, Blountstown has been the county seat since about 1800.

Calhoun County sheriff's deputy Glenn Kimbrel brings us our first grisly tale from the jail. As he tells it, his uncle George used to work for the sheriff's department and tell him stories of all the strange happenings in and around the jail. For example, his uncle told him about a prisoner who, back in 1942, was put in a cell by himself. Not long after he was settled into the cell, deputies heard screams and cries for help coming from the cell upstairs.

When they arrived at the prisoner's cell, it looked like something from a slasher movie. Blood was splattered everywhere. There was even blood dripping from the ceiling. And the man who had walked in under his own power about an hour before lay in his bunk. *Dead*. But the strangest thing was still to come. When they pulled the sheet off him, he was covered in bite marks. And though they investigated, there were no leads or reasonable explanation for what they found in the cell.

In fact, the strange death remains a mystery today.

That's not the end of the story, however. The old jail was finally torn down and a new one built in the same place. Today, it's not unusual for inmates and locals alike to report hearing terrifying screams from the site. Which makes you wonder . . . though the building is gone, do the spirits still linger? What do you think?

Imogene Theater

They say good things come in small packages. Well . . . so do scary things. The Imogene Theater is a good example. Once called The Milton Opera House, it was renamed for Imogene Gooch when her parents bought it in 1921, and it has had an interesting "life" apart from any of its haunted elements. The downstairs has been used as a post office and retail store. However, there was a stretch when the downstairs remained empty for forty years before the Santa Rosa Historical Society acquired it to house the Museum of Local History.

Even today, the theater is the only three-story building in Milton, Florida. It was recently sold to a church group (this ought to be interesting). And even though it was pretty dilapidated in 1909, it was saved from being torn down by a large group of people gathered around it chanting, "Save the Imogene . . . Save the Imogene . . . Save the Imogene . . ." Oddly enough, buildings on either side of it were on fire at the time.

But our story gets interesting back when the theater was still used as a theater. Paranormal investigators and employees tell a pretty convincing story about . . . well . . . let's let them tell it. Tammy Misner, a paranormal investigator formerly working in this area of Florida, conducted an investigation in 2018.

Armed with an Ovilus (a mini-computer that ghosts can use to communicate with the living), a thermal camera, a K2 meter (it activates when a spiritual energy is close by), a structured light sensor (used for detecting visual energy), and divining rods (pair of copper dowels that those on the "other side" can control when they're held by a living person). She came well equipped with both technology and knowledge of the building.

"Legend has it that the little girl, Imogene, performed on the stage the first night her family owned the theater," Misner said. "People have said they've seen her ghost, the height of a child, still dancing on the stage." She has also been seen in other parts of the building.

One experience, shared by a former employee

who did not want his name published, adds credence to the spooky tales of the unexplained in the theater. On one particular night, he was walking through the theater after everyone else was gone. Workers renovating part of the building had left for the day. So, when the gentleman walked to the center of the stage area, he was completely alone. As he scanned the empty seats of the theater, his breath caught in his throat and he felt a chill race along his spine.

There, in the rear of the seating area, stood a child. Or more accurately, the silhouette of a child. As he watched in horror, the image faded, and he heard the sound of footsteps running past him. He moved to the edge of the stage, heart hammering in his chest as he looked all around the area. There was nothing there. Then someone (or something) whispered in his right ear, "Gotcha!" The man ran to the door, locked it behind himself, and ran to his car.

Kyle Verner, the theater's general manager, hears from people on a regular basis who have had paranormal experiences. "We've had six different people, none of whom know each other, describe a gentleman walking the balcony area dressed the exact same way, and all at different times, when there was nobody in the building," he said. "We don't know who he is, but we have suspicions."

How about you? What would YOU do if you came across this ghostly visitor?

Quincy Leaf Theater
Quincy, Florida

Quincy Leaf Theater

While we're on the subject of theaters, let me tell you a tale about the theater visitor who wasn't really there. (Or was he?) A guest of the Quincy Leaf Theater was invited to watch a rehearsal of *Fiddler on the Roof*, and got much more of a show than expected.

"Back in 2007, I visited this theater with a friend who was in a version of *Fiddler on the Roof* and during a rehearsal night, he was allowed to sit up in the balcony to watch. About a third of the way through, I heard someone rattling a doorknob that was on the outside wall and went to open it for them, but I saw it had a steel bar bolted across the threshold and a chain from the doorknob to a bracket on the wall.

"So, I told them the door was sealed from inside and that I could not open it. They stopped and I returned to watch [the show]. Several times through the rest of the show it happened again, and I thought it was someone playing a joke on me since I had been told the place was haunted . . . At the end of the rehearsal, I went back down and approached my friend's group and laughed, telling them they got me with their joke. After a few strange looks, I explained what I meant, and everyone's eyes grew big and a few mouths opened.

"The stage manager told me that was not possible. He took me outside the side stage door and showed me a large open space and a sole door high on the wall. He said the staircase had collapsed well over thirty years ago and that two people were killed in the fall. There was no physical way to reach the door from the outside without an extension ladder or lift platform."

The theater opened in 1949 with cowboy star Roy Rogers as the first headliner, so it was a big deal. Even so, by 1980 the theater was closed . . . but not for long. A few years later, The Quincy Music Group reopened the venue, and they are producing musicals there to this day. But did they know about its haunted history? If not, they do now.

Employees and visitors to The Quincy Leaf Theater have reported hearing footsteps in empty spaces and disembodied voices. Some people even talk about being gripped by a sudden overwhelming feeling of paranoia. And, on more

than one occasion, employees and visitors have seen a man named Mr. McDaniel sitting in the front row. Now that in itself isn't unusual. He is, after all, the theater's former projectionist. So, he probably wants to enjoy the show like everybody else.

The problem is, he's dead. Has been for a while. So yeah, he has made the transition from former employee to paranormal resident. He's not harming anybody, unless scaring the Dickens out of some unsuspecting passer-by counts. As a matter of fact, some of the spirits are rather helpful. One particular Youtuber who does costuming for musicals has found some of the undead "residents" to be a help. On a number of occasions, while carrying heavy boxes of costumes to various parts of the building, the costumer has been guided gently down the stairs by an unseen force.

Maybe it *was* Mr. McDaniel. After all, being dead is no excuse for not lending a helping hand.

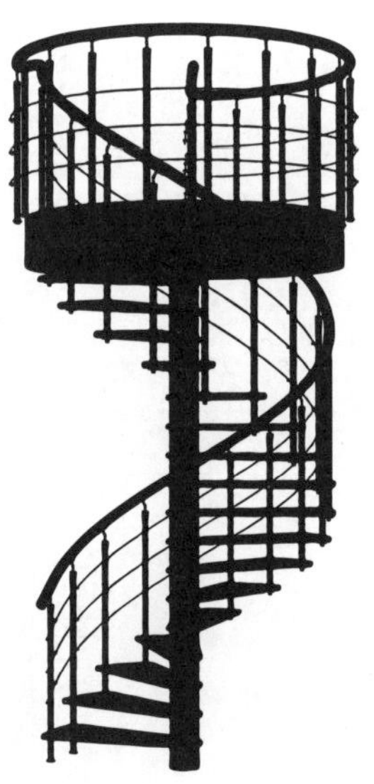

Heading Into the Great Outdoors

We've been cramped up in musty old theaters, jails, hotels, and even a haunted castle long enough. Let's take a walk outside and get a breath of fresh air. We'll get away from ghosts, unseen spectral forces, and members of the undead population who pop up when you least expect it. We should be safe from all that for a while. You know, as long as we don't go near any cemeteries, haunted forests, creepy bridges, or mysterious camping areas.

Yeah . . . I didn't think you were buying the whole "we'll be safer outdoors" idea. No character in any horror movie I know of said that and lived happily ever after. But why are the outdoors so spooky?

Well, when you think about it, cemeteries are pretty easy to figure out. I mean, that's where dead folks hang out. And most of them really are resting in peace. But others had a harder life, a more terrifying death, or they have some kind of serious unfinished business to tend to. And in some cases, like old Indigenous burial grounds, disturbing a resting place of the dead, if it's not done with dignity and respect, *IS* going to come back to haunt you.

Yes, I know that was a bad pun. But if you read my other *Spooky America* book, *The Ghostly Tales of the Haunted North Carolina Coast*, you knew it was coming sooner or later. But seriously, it's almost silly to ask why cemeteries are haunted. That one's easy to figure out. Oddly enough, though, I know about an archway over the entrance of a cemetery in another state that cries bloody tears.

But only on the day of a funeral. Other times it is just a beautiful stone arch. Still, when a funeral procession comes through the arch, people who know the story will bring an umbrella (even when it's not raining) because the legends say that if the bloody colored "tears" from the archway fall on someone, they will be the next to die. Why? Nobody knows. But they're not taking any chances.

That still leaves the question of how a forest (or just a section of it) can be the site of unexplained phenomenon or a haunting. One forest I know of has been the site of a number of UFO sightings and

is believed to be a portal to another dimension, causing visitors to disappear.

Sometimes a forest grows around the site of an abandoned town or village, and the spirits linked

to the town become linked to the forest. Also, just like buildings, a forest can be the place where a horrible accident (or maybe it wasn't an accident) occurred, and the paranormal energy remains.

Some woods seem to be overrun with ghostly presences, UFO sightings, poltergeist activity, orbs, and fireball sightings. And the best answer anyone can offer is the area is cursed. Maybe due to dark rituals, or murder. But sometimes there is no answer that we can pinpoint. Sometimes the only answer is, *it can't be explained.*

So, as long as we're already out here, let's visit the local graveyard.

Coon Hill Cemetery

You know, some people are just rude. You've met people like that before, haven't you? I think we all have. But some ghosts are rude, too. After all, they were people before they became ghosts, spirits, revenants, or whatever undead thing they became. And being dead doesn't help the situation. So, if you ever decide to visit Coon Hill Cemetery, just be warned: one of the cemetery's residents has a bit of an attitude problem.

Why? Nobody really knows. But let's look at the cemetery's history and see if that gives us a clue.

You don't get the reputation as one of the most haunted sites in the county without a good reason.

In 1835, the Second Seminole War began (an effort to move the Seminole people off their land), and in 1842, Santa Rosa County was created. Coon Hill Cemetery has been a part of the county since 1820. There are a number of interesting people buried there, including fifteen Civil War soldiers, three postmasters, two circuit riding preachers (Methodist clergy assigned to travel around specific territories to minister to settlers and organize congregations in the late 1700s and early 1800s), two tax assessors, and one of Florida's first Senators.

The cemetery, surrounded by hundreds of acres of timberland, is located at the end of a mile-long dirt road. The remote area lies between the towns of Chumuckla and Jay. Interestingly, the cemetery is surrounded by a four-foot-high concrete wall. The wall was constructed approximately one hundred years ago to protect the wooden grave markers from fires, which had previously destroyed most of the original markers. Today, only one wooden marker, believed to be 200 years old, still remains.

But let's get back to that wall because it plays an important part in our story. Locals will tell you about playing Humpty Dumpty with the spirits in the cemetery. The game is simple. There is an iron gate at the entrance to the cemetery. Climb on top of the wall next to the gate and walk along the top to the other side. If you walk all the way to the other side of the wall, past all the graves, you win.

Sounds easy. But there's a problem. A sort of *presence* makes itself known in the cemetery. You will walk through cold spots. People have reported hearing a kind of chattering in the background. Many people playing the game have been distracted by a woman calling to them from the emptiness around the tombstones. And there are children. Singing. Or humming. Or chanting the Humpty Dumpty nursery rhyme.

Often, a mist or fog rolls in out of nowhere and surrounds the cemetery. But many people who have played the game say the most unnerving of all is what happens if you make it beyond the first turn in the wall. They have felt something tugging at their ankles, as if it wants them to fall. And if that doesn't work, something may try to *shove* you off the wall. And sure, I know stories like this are filled with anonymous sources. So, I contacted Rick Loe, the founder of Pensacola Paranormal Society (http://pensacolaparanormalsociety.com) to hear what he has to say about the night they conducted an investigation in the cemetery. He and his team originally went the cemetery to explore the mysterious orbs that sometimes appear in photos, but they got more than they bargained for.

This incident comes directly from their investigation notes (the investigators used a K-2 EMF detector to detect electro-magnetic fields/ electrical energy): *This device has five lights, which indicate the strength of the field near the device . . . While walking near one gravesite, the detector gave a five-light reading for nearly ten seconds. Very exciting!*

While exploring the area, Sharon and Taffney [two investigators with the society] *experienced several strange occurrences: Sounds of footsteps in the grass that also moved, sticks being flung from outside of the cemetery, cold spots, and unexplainable sounds.*

"Coon Hill Cemetery was one of the most intense investigations we ever did," Rick said. "The moment we stepped through the gate, it felt like walking into an invisible wall of resistance—like someone was trying to keep us out. We're not new to ghost stories, but that place had a heaviness to it. When our K-2 EMF meter pegged all five lights near a grave and stayed lit for a good ten seconds, it definitely got our attention. And those sounds—footsteps where there were no people, sticks moving when no one was there . . . yeah, that place sticks with you."

Tate's Hell State Forest

This stretch of forest in Carrabelle, Florida is as beautiful as any other in the state. But it also stands as a reminder of the dangers of not keeping your word. Our tale of madness, mayhem, a pig, and a horrific trip through the swamp takes place during the Civil War era. What, you may ask, does all of this have to do with the perils of fibbing? Well, it all started with a Civil War veteran named Jebediah Tate, his half-Cherokee wife, and their son Cebe.

After the Civil War ended, Jebediah bought 160 acres of land (for $5) in Sumatra, Florida as a homestead. Cebe helped his father clear land, collect pine oil, take care of their livestock, and do all the other hard work involved in making the land livable. Unfortunately, in the midst of the hard work and sacrifice, Cebe's mother died from yellow fever. Jebediah and his son were very sad, and over the months that followed, things began to fall apart. The house, the family, their livestock business.

After months of wondering what he was going to do, the father made a trip deep into the woods

to see an Indigenous medicine man. Maybe he could tell the soldier-turned-farmer why his luck was suddenly sour. The medicine man listened carefully, then told the farmer he could help him. They made an agreement that Jebediah would give the medicine man a pig every year. He also had to promise not to enter the medicine man's sanctified part of the forest again. In exchange, he would reverse the farmer's bad luck and make his farmland prosperous once again.

For the next three years, the medicine man would come to the farm on a specific day to receive his pig. And for three years, the farm prospered as

never before. However, in 1874, Jebediah decided he didn't want to give the old man his pig. The medicine man stood for a moment and before he turned to leave, he cursed the two men and their land: "Since you broke our agreement, you will not only see hard times, you will go through hell."

That very year, Cebe's father died from malaria. The pine trees gave very little oil. The sugar cane wouldn't grow, and the cows began to disappear. But the pigs thrived so much that Cebe had to build two more pens to hold them all. Still, his bad luck continued and the farm continued to fail. The one bright spot in his otherwise hard life was his new wife. Despite the bad luck with the farm, in 1875,

the young man had married a beautiful woman, and for the most part, they were happy.

The only problem? She was Jewish and followed her religion's kosher dietary laws, so eating pork was not an option. Because pigs were the only livestock on the farm, she ate corn, potatoes, and pancakes with molasses—but that was no substitute for meat. When she had ignored the situation as long as she could, she told Cebe she wanted some beef. So, he took his hunting dogs, his shotgun, and went into the forest to see if he could find any of his missing cows . . . or any other cow for that matter.

A day or so into his hunt, his dogs ran off to chase a panther. And at some point, he lost his shotgun in the mud. More tired than he had ever been in his life, Cebe wandered into a stand of Dwarf Cyprus trees to rest and escape the bugs. But this was the very part of the woods that the old medicine man had told the boy and his father never to enter. And he was now sleeping in the forbidden woods.

A sharp pain woke Cebe, and he jerked awake just in time to see a large poisonous snake slithering into the swamp and swimming away. The pain was unbelievable, but the young man decided he had to keep moving. So, he forced himself to stand, and he started walking again.

Delirious from lack of food and the murky swamp water he had been drinking—and in horrible pain—Cebe stumbled through the woods until he finally reached a clearing near Carrabelle. He had been lost for about seven days, and he must have been a sight when he met two men coming

from the other direction. Dirty, disheveled, and barely able to hold himself upright, he fell down in front of the men and lived just long enough to murmur, "My name is Cebe Tate, and I just came through Hell."

That's a pretty compelling "coincidence" don't you think? The old medicine man's curse played out in real life. While there aren't any stories of orbs, spectral images, or the form of an old shaman watching from the woods, it has been said that some people who have ventured deep into the woods of the Florida Panhandle were never heard from again—and others who *did* return came back with serious injuries. Moral of the story? Always keep your word. And remember: when someone tells you to stay out of a forbidden forest . . . you might want to listen.

Camp Helen State Park
Inlet Beach, Florida

Camp Helen State Park

Wow! That was some tale. Can you imagine being lost in the swamp and woods for seven days? Why don't we make our way to another state park; one without all the bugs, poisonous snakes, and medicine man curses. Camp Helen State Park comes to mind. It is located in the southernmost part of Walton County in a very pretty place called Inlet Beach. In fact, the state park has a lodge and twelve cottages that are maintained all year long. The buildings and surroundings are so beautiful, the lodge has been the site of many weddings throughout the years.

The park is tranquil and serene, with its winding paths, moss-draped trees, and the calming sounds of the Gulf. So much so that many visitors are completely unaware of its tragic haunted history. The state of Florida has been in charge of the property since 1997. But the park's ghostly history goes back well before that.

Truth be told, it goes back to the creation of the park's home, Okaloosa County, in 1824. Back in the days of steam trains and riverboats, both were important in the lumber and timber industry. And those industries created many jobs and a better way of life for the locals.

Local historian Emily Smith is very familiar with Camp Helen's tragic history. She says that the park's first ghost is Rose, a young slave girl killed by Indigenous people in 1843. Smith said Rose was a passenger on a ship that ran aground during a New Year's Eve storm. The captain and his crew tried to make friends with the local Indigenous community, and at first, they seemed friendly.

But one day, when the captain was out looking for food, the group attacked. In the skirmish, Rose was killed and buried in a shallow grave. But she wasn't alone. When the captain returned, he too was killed, as were many of his crew. Witnesses say that on moonlit nights, you can sometimes see Rose as she walks along the beaches. The captain has also been seen walking the trails and even appeared in the camp's log cabin. (According to the person who witnessed the ghostly sight, the captain claimed that the cabin was his.)

Avondale Mills owned the property in 1945, and they had given a room to one of their VIP visitors. According to park ranger Clayton Iron Wolf, during the night "... he was awakened by a male figure that, for some reason, they decided was the visage of Captain Phillips, and he was telling the visitor to get out of his house. That this was *his* house."

[Author's Note: If I had been in the cabin, it really would have been his. Along with my suitcase and anything else I left behind as I ran out the door.]

To this day, a young boy can often be seen on or near the pier closest to the house—the same spot where he fell into the water more than a century ago. Unfortunately, he could not swim. But park ranger Iron Wolfe had the full story here, too. "The little boy was named George. He was the grandchild of Mrs. Margaret Hicks, one of the builders of this home, and he passed away when he was very small

while he was down here visiting his grandmother. George will usually be playing by the dock. But he has also been heard walking around the upstairs of the cabin."

Not all encounters are quite so easygoing, however. One person who wants to remain anonymous has an interesting encounter story. She and her fiancé (now her husband) had visited the area on a previous trip. They were so impressed with the beauty and the lodge facilities, that they decided to have their wedding at Camp Helen. So, in October of 2015, they came back with their families and friends.

After the rehearsal dinner, the groom and groomsmen went to the bachelor party. The bride and bridesmaids stayed at the lodge and got ready for the bachelorette party. The women were downstairs in the lodge, dancing to their favorite songs. Snacks, punch, fancy decorations, gifts, and lively music all added to the party atmosphere. Until all of a sudden, the music stopped. Everyone looked around, trying to see who had shut off the Bluetooth speaker. One of the bridesmaids, frustrated with the seeming joke said out loud, "Okay. Quit messing with the music."

Suddenly, a man appeared in the corner of the room. His eyes blazed in anger. He pointed at the group and said, "Get out of my home. Now!" He continued to stare at them with hate-filled eyes. The bride pulled out her phone and called 9-1-1 to report that someone who wasn't supposed to be there had had broken into the park. As the other women frantically called family and friends, the room went dark. The women began to scream.

Within moments, a park ranger rushed in, his flashlight a welcome beacon. He flipped the switch and the room flooded with light. "Why were you all standing around in the dark, screaming?" he asked. They told him what happened, and he looked around the property but didn't see anything out of the ordinary. Still, the women stayed with their families in the rented condos instead of sticking with the sleeping arrangements at the lodge.

The next day, the wedding went off perfectly. There were tears of joy, lots of hugs, and well wishes for the happy couple. Their day could not have been better. And they felt that way until the pictures arrived from the photographer. The newly married husband and wife laughed and cried over the wonderful photographs. That is, until one particular photograph surfaced. The woman gasped and sat perfectly still.

There, in one of the group family photos, was a familiar face. Staring back at her was the "man" who had invaded her bachelorette party. Brows furrowed, his hate-filled eyes blazing.

Bellamy Bridge

Anyone who follows the half-mile long Bellamy Bridge Heritage Trail will find themselves in one of nature's beautiful wonderlands. Located off State Road 162 in Mariana, just west of the Chipola River, the trail is home to towering trees, luxuriant foliage, and many rare and endangered plants. Additionally, the route provides prime access to the Upper Chipola WMA, a stop on the Great Florida Birding Trail.

However, these are not the only amazing things to be found along the relatively short walk. The trail also leads to the remains of a bridge. This bridge is special because it was built in 1914, making it one of the oldest structures of its kind in Florida. But its fame doesn't stop there.

Because the Bellamy Bridge is haunted.

Now, that shouldn't be a surprise. This is, after all, a book about haunted places. So, what makes this abandoned bit of history so special? On more than one occasion, it has been designated as the most haunted spot in Florida.

The bridge's dark history dates back centuries. In March of 1818, a bloody battle took place at the bridge's current location in Upper Chipola.

Brigadier general William McIntosh and his troops attacked refugee camps in Ekanachatte ("Red Ground" in the Creek language). At the conclusion of what became known as the Battle of the Upper Chipola, an important battle of the First Seminole War, 180 men, women, and children had been captured and brought back to McIntosh's camp. The siege and its terrible bloodshed were just the beginning of the bridge's chilling history.

In 1836, Dr. Edward C. Bellamy and his wife Ann Bellamy purchased the land and made the area their home. His brother, Dr. Samuel C. Bellamy, lived nearby. Samuel was a planter, politician, and bank examiner. He was also in love with a beautiful woman named Elizabeth.

The two were deeply in love and were married in the backyard of a beautiful mansion that Dr. Bellamy had built for his wife-to-be in nearby Marianna. Stories vary, but after the ceremony, during the wedding party festivities, Elizabeth was either dancing with her husband or sitting in a chair between dances when her long gown suddenly came in contact with either a candle or an open fireplace.

Her dress burst into flames and Elizabeth ran screaming from the house. Horribly injured, she survived for only a few days. Her body was taken to the plantation of Samuel's brother, and she was laid to rest in a grove of trees near the Chipola River. But even death could not claim her completely. Shortly after her funeral, a ghostly figure in white appeared near the spot where she was buried. And years later, when the bridge was built, her ghost could be seen in the swamp near the bridge.

About fifteen years after the tragic wedding, Dr. Horace Ely and Bird B. Hathaway built a wooden bridge on Bellamy's land. The bridge served as an important crossing point for a new road that stretched from Campbellton to Port

Jackson—and became the site of many tragic events. Take the story of three cousins, for example.

Dan Smith, Sylvester Hart, and Levi Hart were moonshiners. That means they made illegal alcohol, and often such people worked at night (by the light of the *moon*), so law enforcement officers couldn't find them. One night, Dan was counting jars of moonshine and thought some was missing. He told Levi, because they both knew their cousin, Sylvester, was not an honest person. They suspected that he stole it. On May 9, 1914, Levi shot Sylvester. Not long after that, a husband and wife had an argument that got out of hand quickly. The wife said she was going to take their daughter and leave him.

But before she could leave, the husband took their daughter for a ride in their wagon. The little girl had no idea what her father had planned. When he came to the Bellamy Bridge, he stopped the horse and did a horrible thing. A day or so later, their bodies were discovered in the wagon, out by the bridge.

No location can be the site of such dark energy and remain completely normal. To this day, people talk about their encounters with the supernatural near the bridge. Sometimes it's a feeling of dread as they approach the bridge. Some have heard screams and cries near the bridge when no one is nearby. Others have seen a woman in white in the swamp near the site. But before we move on, I'll tell you about Carl Pence and his experience at the bridge.

One day, as Carl and his family were walking on the trail that leads to the bridge, he began to feel uneasy. Almost as if something was . . . stalking them. As they were standing at the posts of the steel bridge, Carl realized his phone and other electronic equipment were dead, despite having charged everything earlier. Then, all of a sudden, his daughter, Emma, started looking around frantically. When he asked what was wrong, she said someone had been speaking to her.

They spent over ten minutes checking the surrounding area, but as far as they could tell, they were completely alone. Everything was clear. However, when they left the bridge and headed back to the parking lot, Carl Pence said he again felt that same uneasy feeling of being stalked. To this day, he is not sure what they came across at the Bellay Bridge. Could someone—or *something*—still be out there, waiting in the shadows for the bridge's next unsuspecting visitor? Only time will tell.

Double Bridge of Holmes Creek

Hey fellow ghost hunters, are you still with me? I thought you would be. Since we're all still here together, I think we have time for one more story. This one is also about a bridge, but it's not so much spooky as it is just plain *weird*. How weird you may ask? Do you know what a Skunk Ape is? Well, hang on, because we're headed into some odd territory.

If you're traveling Highway 77 toward Graceville, keep your eyes peeled (ouch!). That stretch of road is loaded with hauntings and other strange occurrences. So, let's take a look at some local history. First, the county was created on January 8, 1848, becoming Florida's twenty-seventh county.

It is said to have been named for two very important people: Chief Holmes, a Creek leader, and North Carolina settler Thomas J. Holmes. Chief Holmes settled there in the early 1800s. Unfortunately, he was killed in the First Seminole War of 1818. Thomas Holmes arrived about 1830.

If you continue on Highway 77, turn down Piano Road, and keep twisting and turning, you will come to a desolate wooden double bridge (two bridges built side-by-side). Locals say the creek has a certain unnatural energy that can be felt when you cross the creek, or are just in the vicinity. The woods and swamps that surround the bridges are the natural habitat of an unusual creature: the skunk ape. And what exactly is a skunk ape? Excellent question.

They are large and legendary (and very hairy) human-like creatures that some people say live in the forests and swamps in the southeast part of North America; mostly in Florida. Skunk apes particularly like swampy areas like the Everglades or Myakka State Park. And hoo-boy do they stink! A skunk ape smells like a cross between a skunk (get it . . . *skunk* ape) and rotten eggs.

The mythical skunk ape has been referred to as the "cousin" of the northwest's famous Bigfoot. And while the Florida relative is an elusive creature, it's not shy. Waylon Moore can vouch for that fact. He lives near the bridges and hears grunts and knocks around his property, especially at night. But one night in particular, the legends became real.

About a half hour before sunset, Waylon realized he hadn't seen his dog, Buck, for a long time. Which was strange because his dog, his buddy, was always with him. But now Buck was missing. Waylon called for his dog over and over, but no response. Thinking that his dog might have gone down to the water, Waylon headed toward the creek, his calls for Buck becoming more frantic. Because that creek was bad news.

"*Buck . . . Buck . . .*" he called over and over as he came to the first bridge. No response. When he called the third time, Waylon was relieved to hear a faint bark and the jingling of a dog collar. But the sound abruptly stopped, replaced by the deepest, most horrifying growl he had ever heard. The sound made every hair on his neck stand up.

A moment later, the creek and the surrounding forest fell completely silent. Waylon's heart pounded in the eerie quiet. Then, something nudged his leg.

It was Buck, but his collar was gone. The dog was hunkered down low on the ground, quivering in fear. He whined and continued to tremble. Waylon comforted Buck as best he could, then said, "C'mon boy. Let's go home." Buck stood on shaky legs, and they started walking home slowly and carefully. But then they heard it—fast movement crashing through the brush behind them. Waylon yelled, "Go!" and he and Buck took off for home at a full sprint, not slowing down until Waylon slammed the door behind them and they were safe inside.

After a while, Buck settled down, and the two of them sat on the couch for a while. A fire crackled in the hearth, and they were both nearly asleep when something thudded against the sliding glass door at the rear of the house. *Hard*. Waylon grabbed his shotgun and swept through the entire house, checking every room and corner. Then he went outside and carefully checked the perimeter. When he was certain that whatever had pounded on his door was gone, he locked up and eventually went to bed. To this day, he says it was the scariest night of his life.

But not every unusual event in the area has to do with the famous cryptid of the swamps. Sarah McCoy has a different but equally terrifying tale to tell. She and a few of her braver friends were curious about the legend of the Woman in Green. According to local legend, anybody who gets close to the creek near the bridge in the dead of night will witness a terrifying sight—the lady in green who floats in the muddy creek below.

So, one night, Sarah and a few friends walked down the dirt road that leads to the two bridges. She thought, *This darkness and fog would spook anybody.* Sarah looked at her friends and asked, "Are y'all feeling a little uneasy?" One of the friends replied, "Yeah, I almost feel like we shouldn't be here." But they continued their walk to the bridges anyway.

Oddly enough, the moment they arrived at the bridges, the women heard a loud knock. Thinking it was just the old bridge settling, they ignored the sound and sat together at the base of the bridge. Then they concentrated on staying calm and watching the creek. Soon, they saw a greenish glow in the distance, and continued to watch as it moved closer and closer. Little by little, they began to make out the figure of a beautiful woman shrouded in green, floating just above the water. It was true! The old legend was real.

The figure continued to float down the river,

and as it passed under the bridges, the women leaned over to continue watching. Suddenly, the figure lunged straight up toward them. As the friends fell backward in terror, the woman's green face began to change. In an instant, they were staring at the twisted face of an old hag, screaming at them with rage. *"What are you doing here?"*

The women closed their eyes and quaked, their hearts racing. All around them came the sound of people gathering—footsteps, whispers, movement in the darkness. Then, there was silence. Sarah slowly opened her eyes. The figure was gone. The normal night sounds had returned, and they could hear the gentle flow of water below. Without a word, the friends knew it was time to go home.

No one spoke on the return trip. When they arrived at Sarah's house, the three friends sat in stunned silence, each one trying to figure out what had just happened. After a time, the women started talking about what they witnessed on the double bridge. But as they compared their experiences, something strange emerged—*all three had seen something completely different* when they looked at the Woman in Green.

And no one knows why.

A Ghostly Goodbye

First, thank you for buying this book (or for standing in the store reading it). I appreciate every one of you. And if this book (or any of my books) makes you want to explore any part of this Spooky America we live in, let me give you a little advice:

Always take a friend. If something starts chasing you, you need to have somebody with you that you can outrun. (Just kidding. It's really just safer that way.) So, use the buddy system. Seriously, it ALWAYS pays to be safe.

Be sure to ask permission before you start exploring a building, cemetery, or other spooky location. Not every place is open to the public. But some places will be open to you if you ask politely.

Make sure you let an adult know where you are going, who you are going with, and when you will be back.

Be sure to take the essentials: Water, a flashlight, a small first aid kit, a snack, pen and notebook, and a smartphone.

If you have access to professional ghost hunting equipment, bring an EMF Meter (measures

fluctuations in the magnetic field that could be caused by ghostly apparitions), digital recorder, digital thermometer, and walkie-talkies. If you don't have an EMF meter, a compass works, too. Just watch for the needle to move erratically.

So, that's it for our journey through the spooky Florida Panhandle! I appreciate you being part of the adventure. And I look forward to seeing you again on our next ghost hunt.

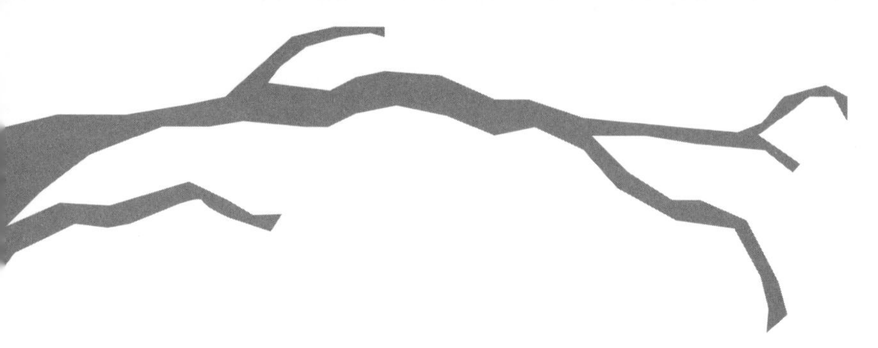

Acknowledgments

Thank you to Jessica Rothenberg (my editor), Jessica Nevins (my designer), and the *Spooky America* team. You all rock, and I can't wait to start the next spooky book.

Thank you to paranormal investigator and founder of the Pensacola Paranormal Society (http://pensacolaparanormalsociety.com), Rick Loe for his help and insights into this haunted part of Florida.

And thank you to Katlyn Jones for writing *Haunted Florida Panhandle*. Who knew the panhandle was so creepy!

Bibliography

https://www.floridahauntedhouses.com/

https://www.wjhg.com/content/news/Meet-the-ghosts-of-Camp-Helen-State-Park-564071811.html

Rick Loe interview (founder of Pensacola Paranormal Society. http://pensacolaparanormalsociety.com)

THOMAS SMITH has been a writer for many years, and his favorite stories are the spooky ones. If it has haunted houses, creepy graveyards, ghost ships, or specters in the moonlight, he'll read it. He even lived in a haunted house for a couple of years (but the ghost was friendly, so they got along fine). Now he lives at the beach in Florida with his wife, six guitars, and a sock monkey named Ray.

Check out some of the other *Spooky America* titles available now!

Spooky America was adapted from the creeptastic *Haunted America* series for adults. *Haunted America* explores historical haunts in cities and regions across America. Here's more from the original *Haunted Florida Panhandle* author, Katlyn Jones:

www.instagram.com/authorkatlynjones